Behind the Blue Edge
of the Sea

For Marcia and Jim—
who both love poetry
and each other.
I hope you enjoy
my little book.
Love,
Judy

Behind the Blue Edge
of the Sea

poems by
Judith L. Shaffer

Poetic Justice Books
Port St. Lucie, Florida

Printed in the United States of America.
Published by Poetic Justice Books
Port Saint Lucie, Florida
www.poeticjusticebooks.com

ISBN: 978-1-950433-49-0

FIRST EDITION
10 9 8 7 6 5 4 3 2 1

For Larry,
who knows poetry should be read aloud

contents

Behind the Blue Edge
of the Sea

I

Family Vacations

My childhood holidays
were spent driving to
historic destinations;
each an educational event.

Father designed every trip
with engineering precision,
never leaving home without
his Triple A Trip Tik map.

He proudly commanded the helm
of his large shiny black Packard,
complete with running boards
and clean white-wall tires.

Mother sat calmly off to his right,
my brother and I in back,
endlessly following the flying swan
perched on the nose of the hood.

Traveling black ribbons of road,
imagination flew along with the swan,
while Mother's rhythmic voice
filled those hours reciting poems.

She knew hundreds by heart,
each painted a picture in words.
Mother left me this legacy,
an enduring love of poetry.

Horses

Trained as a farrier when he was young, now he is ninety-two.
He always loved the horses
and caring for their hooves.

The Army listed him a blacksmith, served in combat, returned alive.
Never spoke about the war,
felt lucky to have survived.

His health failing, his mind fading, he no longer knows his family.
All day long, he watches
western movies on TV.

Doesn't care about the story or that the good guys won.
He says, *"I only watch because
I love to see the horses run."*

The Man Without a Nose

Howard O'Neal was an old man
who'd spent his entire life
upon the island of Ocracoke
off the North Carolina coast.
Working on the ferry
that plied the waters in between

Hatteras Island and his home,
when he was just sixteen,
he suffered a grievous injury
on that ferry one dark night -
a blast disfigured his young face
and took away his nose.

I heard he was a carver
who sculpted small shorebirds,
like those who ran upon the sands
of the beach at Ocracoke.
I made the journey down the coast
to meet this humble man

who endured an isolated life
in a cottage edged by the sound.
He was genuinely delighted
I had come to see his carvings
and showed me how he made them
from bits of scavenged wood.

His hands were scarred from cutting
and polishing his birds,
using handmade tools to craft
his graceful Sanderlings.
Admiring all his work, I asked
to buy a number of his flock.

Pleased at my request,
he noddingly concurred.
His birds were lovely to behold
posed on little blocks of wood,
heads facing to the salty wind
each bird stood very still -

and every single one of them
possessed a long and slender bill.

Messages

I heard the story of a young boy,
whose father was deployed to a war
waging in a faraway land.

Before he left, he told his son
he would send messages to the moon
only the boy could hear.

The news came later that year.
His father had been felled on the battlefield
by fire from the enemy's hand.

Now when the nights are clear,
his son can often be found
standing out under the stars,

head tilted back, eyes fixed on that shining sphere -
one small hand raised,
cupped upward around his ear.

The Student
(To Ruth Oglesby)

She works the daytime shift routine
with little time to spare,
an unknown cog in the machine,
bent to a job that leads nowhere.

She moves along in quietude
in the constant factory blare,
wrapped in her silent, pensive mood
and so the world is unaware

that on her own at fifty-nine,
she has the fortitude to dare
to learn to read and write each line
found in her book of prayer.

Each class attended does impress
upon her mind new thoughts to share.
She's warmed by feelings of success
and full of hope beyond compare.

She leaves each weekly lesson filled
with knowledge that supplants despair
and walks toward home, instilled
with unaccustomed pride to wear.

No passerby sets her apart,
nor even sees her there.
But I see courage in her heart
and roses in her hair.

Honor
South Carolina 1987

Alone I drive a country road
on a shining green spring day,
a smudge of clouds above,
scent of freshly turned earth in the air.

Unable to pass a slanted fedora
driving a dusty old car,
I slow to his pace, until he pulls off
onto the grassy shoulder.

Thinking he might have a problem,
I proceed to do the same,
as a string of dark cars moves ever so slowly
toward us in the oncoming lane.

The man in the hat steps out of his car
when the funeral cortege approaches.
No town nearby, he could not possibly know
this soul so recently departed.

Yet there he stands, hat in his hand,
held reverently over his heart.

Barriers

Late in the days of détente,
my husband and I were requested,
by the medical company where he was employed,
to entertain a doctor from Moscow
visiting on diplomatic exchange.

She had asked us to show her our nation's capital.
So we picked her up at her DC hotel,
greeting her as she entered our car
and discovered she spoke no English.
(our Russian was limited to da and nyet).

But proudly we showed her the sights,
the soaring Washington Monument,
the White House, the Capitol, the National Mall,
our noble Lincoln Memorial.
And last on our tour - the dark Vietnam Wall.

We stood quietly beside the long list of names,
her eyes leaking pain, she tried to explain
our Vietnam had been her Afghanistan.
By the end of the day we were weary
of abstract hand signals and gestures.

As the sun sank beyond the Potomac,
we strolled silently across a broad field
toward our car parked off in the distance.
Glancing down, I noticed a daisy
waving in the midst of the grass.

Stopping to pick up the flower,
I gently pulled off two petals
reciting along as I plucked,
the forever girlhood chant -
"he loves me, he loves me not".

She smiled as she took the daisy
from my outstretched hand.
In Russian, she continued on with the verse.
Gazing together at the tattered daisy,
the wall dividing us shattered.

The Tin Man

He has painted
skulls and crossbones
on his black leather
jacket and boots.
His eighteen-year-old
eyes are vacant,
his soul sealed,
contained and aloof.

Drugs,
experiments
in time,
have twisted
his ideas,
scrambling
a fine mind.

The doctors say
he is brilliant,
but no one can
reach any part
of the one
I call the Tin Man,
who has yet
to find his heart.

II

Sweet Dixie Music

Old dark ivy climbs around
a cool stone fountain dripping time,
while I become entwined

with the rhythm of a five piece band;
tossing out sweet Dixieland,
perfumed by oleander

and flung across the brick veranda,
drawing me into a history
of New Orleans I do not know.

Bass notes step in sauntered cadence
with brushing strokes on time-worn drums,
steadily supporting a clear staccato clarinet.

The battered horn pumps out
a well-deep melody, involuntarily
my eyes fill to the brim.

Within the counter harmony of weary melancholy,
I hear a whole hard southern story
from the tarnished slide trombone.

As this music winds together
and overflows the courtyard rim,
it comes out struttin' glory,

pouring happiness on me
in the timeless memory of
"When the Saints Go Marching In."

Morning Song

At sunup I am serenaded
by a joyous Mocking bird,
perched in my Poinciana tree.

His repertoire is limitless,
including every call
he has ever heard.

Not knowing however long
his performance might go on -
causes me to recognize

how temporal life can be,
and his unrecorded aria
is a song I hope will never end.

The Dancer

She fluffs the cup of rabbit fur
to place upon her toes
followed by the lamb's wool
shaped to put on top,
then slides her feet into
satin slippers with wooden toes.

She wraps the satin ribbons
about her ankles tightly
and ties them into place.
Now slips into her costume,
cap sleeves with white satin bodice,
to arrange white clouds of tulle

that fall below her waist.
Finally, she sets a headband
of white feathers on her hair.
She assumes a pose and takes
her place upon the stage;
her feet in fifth position,

wrists gently crossed in front,
fingers gracefully arched,
head bowed. The curtain rises.
As the beautiful
haunting music of
Tchaikovsky fills the air,

her heart is light.
She knows her steps;
relevé, she rises onto her toes,
her arms in fifth position
arched above her head -
tip-tip, tip-tip, tip-tip,

glissade, arabesque,
step, step, jeté, glissade, gran jeté,
she floats into the flock
of the circling corps de ballet.
Melding with the dancers,
she is transformed into a swan.

Carousel

Syncopated music springs
from a hidden calliope.
Shiny mirrors glitter above
reflecting gilded trim.

Round and round the horses ride,
their glass eyes wink and sparkle
amid the dancing light
wrapped in a magic circle.

Happily you scramble on
an elegant black horse,
trimmed with burnished mane and tail,
set in the center lane.

As he begins his canter,
moving up and down,
you clutch the silver pole
in order to hang on.

Next you choose a steady steed,
the white fancy prancing horse,
standing still, head held high
in the very outside lane,

now allowing you a chance,
with every revolution,
to lean way out and snatch
the coveted brass ring.

With arms too short to stretch,
disappointed, you resolve
to return again next year
when you have grown a bit -

to risk that reach
and grasp the prize,
the elusive golden ring.

At the Symphony

The music begins.
As I listen, I'm taken away
in a rudderless boat
that glides down a long green river,
ending in a turquoise bay.

Sails set to go with the wind
whichever way it may blow,
my boat continues beyond the bay,
swept into a dark blue sea.

The melody swells and crests;
daggers of lightning pierce the sky.
Bellowing thunder resounds,
as the rolling waves surge upward.

Like the ocean, my heart rises.
Unbidden, salty tears appear.
When the applause finally dies,
unashamed, I dry my eyes.

Route 17

A grinding tractor trailer,
hugely masked in arched eyebrows,
swept past my little car
at sixty-five and
closely cut in front of me.

A driver peering through his glass
seemed to be trying to decide
how young I might really be.
I was relaxed
enjoying this day's drive

until I noticed another truck
following me quite close behind.
Its macho grill was a leering grin
and I found myself
hemmed in by two long-bed Lotharios.

I rocked in the cradle in between
to laugh at this scenario.
They must have thought I was 17
(who else would drive a red
low slung sports machine?)

Of course they could not see
inside my car, though they could
observe my hand upon the wheel
keeping time to what they
probably surmised was the

driving beat of some hard rock.
Those two would certainly have been
surprised, both at my age,
if they had seen,
and that I was simply listening

to Antonin Dvorak's moving
Symphony No.17.

III

Last Night

You left,
and night fell off
in sapphire pieces,
unstrung against the far end of the sky.

Samba rhythms
swung beyond me,
melting on the phosphorescent tide.

Dawn raised
silent warning fingers -
waves curled in questions that still linger.

Morning breathed out
all the promises
never intended to be kept.

My lost heart
flew off to find last night,
behind the blue edge of the sea

and wept.

Windancer

We sailed northeast out of Marathon Key,
alone on the ocean facing high seas,
our catamaran beating to windward.
Plowing through endless crashing waves,
we plunged forward, pitched sideways,
as if riding the back of a whale.

Seven hours later, with the sun sliding down,
Windancer tucked into shelter
slipping behind Rodriquez Key,
as the sea continued its rush to the west.
Now anchored alee, out of its path,
just a gentle slow motion was left.

After dining on lamb chops
and a glass of champagne,
we four sat down on the deck.
Gazing at the night sky above,
we were all smitten by the sight
of the glorious Milky Way.

Millions of stars lit up the darkness,
so brightly it was hard to discern
our familiarly known constellations.
Overwhelmed by the beauty of boundless stars,
I heard the quiet truth they were whispering -
how utterly insignificant we are.

Encounter

Two dolphins came by late today,
perhaps the same who rode our bow wave yesterday,
to find us as we lay quietly on evening anchor.
We saw them clearly through the blue
Caribbean sea, pulsing closer to explore our boat.
I was compelled to join them in their play.

Escaping from my friends,
I climbed the high edge of the foredeck.
Moments passed as I stood poised to dive -
arms outstretched against a pastel sky.
My shadow mixed in with the rigging,
appearing to the dolphins part of the ketch,

of her tall masts and loosely furled sails
casting lines made longer
by the evening angle of the sun.
Within the shimmering water below
I watched the dolphins roll about
in St. John's Bay.

I hesitated still -
then bravely crashed headlong
into their clear blue world.
Erupting bubbles burst like shattered glass,
fragments glittered slowly past
their compact velvet bodies.

My voice squeaked out a sound I hoped
would seem familiar. The dolphins turned
sweet smiling eyes to gaze at this intruder.
We three hung there transfixed,
suspended lightly in one space,
our minds reached out toward embrace.

The chasm was too great.
Two tails were raised in time,
the dolphins sped away.
I now expelled
what little breath I held
into an empty bowl of crystalline.

Equilibrium

We sail homeward from Bimini,
our son at the helm of his tall-masted catamaran,
just a speck on a darkening ocean.

Conversation and laughter
from our family vacation,
ended, carried off by the wind.

We six sit apart, each gazing westward,
and watch the gold sun drifting down
to rest on a lavender ribbon of cloud.

Turning around, I find a silver full moon,
stealthily risen in the opposite direction,
at precisely the same height as the sun.

Moving up to the deck, I stretch one arm
to the east - the other west,
reaching outward to touch those bright spheres.

The sun glows, the moon smiles,
time holds its breath -
I stand at the fulcrum of yin and yang,

inhaling this moment of perfect balance.

Atonement

September, Nags Head

The gentle sea arises,
awakened by the wind.
His breath grows stronger,
roiling up the sea.
Her waves rise up to meet him
as she pulses to the shore.

He whips her into frenzy.
Facing to the wind,
her spray is caught and blown.
Grimacing, she bares her teeth,
and casts white foam
upon the beach.

The wind has pushed too far,
driving the sea toward
madness. Swells roll up
from her great belly
and spill out uncontrolled,
lashing at the dunes.

To quell her anger,
he sends long sheets of rain,
slicing down across her back.
As her fury now subsides,
she casts out pieces of debris
claimed throughout the storm.

Turning, the wind relaxes.
The sea slows, softly giving
up real treasures now;
whole whelks, lettered olives,
pink scallop shells -
contrite and penitent for her wrath.

He strokes her, as she apologizes,
offering small unbroken gifts;
the fragile wafer of a sand dollar,
a delicate auger wrapped in seaweed
to protect its slender point.

IV

Flying

Once I was a silver Osprey
soaring on the gale,
wings outspread above the sea,
riding on the music of the wind,

sailing on the edge of hurricanes,
rising higher than the gulls,
wheeling, lifting, gliding,
carving out the sky -

    when I was young and beautiful.

Now all the years have passed,
I am become a small brown hen
with wings no longer lifting me,
earthbound,

my head bent down,
pecking for what little
I can find to eat
upon the ground.

    Still -
    at times I lift my head and I remember flying.

Sandhill Cranes
(Originated in Russia, over one million years ago)

The Tsar and his Tsarina
fly from their nearby nest
onto the landing strip
in the field behind our home.
Once on the ground, wings ruffled,
they preen to look their best.
The noble birds approach
with that stately hesitating step
reserved for royalty.

As the pair arrive, I bow,
fill a dish with seeds
and set it on a little stand
so they might eat with ease.
Tsarina is the first to eat,
while behind the Tsar stands watch
through his all-seeing yellow eyes.
Done, she is excused
and he begins to dine.

The court jester squirrel comes near,
but the royal birds are not amused.
They stare and threaten with their wings
to make the squirrel be gone.
When their meal is finished,
both red-crowned heads are bowed
and they resume their stately walk
to inspect the balance of their realm.

This pair has visited us
almost every day this year,
until the midst of April
when they do not appear.
We find where they are nesting
and observe a new-born chick.

We know we will not see them
for several months this spring;
for they will stand by their infant
until the babe can fly.

Two months later the royal pair return.
No youngster comes along with them.
We fear the worst has happened.
Later, we see a furry youngster,
with its bobcat parents nearby.
Perhaps they are the Bolsheviks
who caused the chick's demise.

The Canada Fleet

Here they come again,
the whole flotilla.
Handsome military ships
running smoothly under power.
Gunmetal hulls with bright
white transoms and vigilant eyes
that sweep the lake from
each tall black conning tower.

Thirty-four sail here today.
At the center of the convoy
Mother and Father hover around
eight young cadets, whose long
straight necks hold up proud heads
with new black caps and white chin straps;
standard issue uniform
beneath pubescent down.

They come for crumbs of bread -
the whole armada
driving forward toward my dock.
Upon arriving, most lay back
and now allow the family
to take the closest berths.
So I am instructed
to feed the young ones first.

Mother drives away a mallard.
Father – watching me – swims past,
stretching for a morsel tossed
within his grasp, but gently eases back
as the smallest reaches out to dip
his fuzzy head toward the floating snack.
Then Father flaps one powerful wing
and I salute him back.

Chaos

A stagger of starlings
swoops into that tree,
shrieking and screaming
as they arrive,
announcing
some unknown
emergency.

Settling down,
the crowd hops
to the ground,
chortling and chattering
while they discuss
tasty insects to eat
the flock finds in the dust.

Silent signals are sent,
the dark mob dashes off,
flying swiftly to swarm
in a much larger tree,
declaring once more
another
calamity.

Swallow-Tailed Kites

I have fallen in love with Swallow-Tailed Kites,
the most elegant birds to inhabit the skies,
whose slim white bodies effortlessly glide
beneath four-foot black and white wings.

Rising on tides of wind, a Swallow-Tailed Kite
lifts off from the Pantanal wetlands of Brazil,
where she has spent the winter, to embark on her
arduous journey to fly over five thousand miles.

Retracing the route she followed before,
her long wings slice through the air
to carry her northward, soaring over the Andes,
then on toward Yucatan.

There, she must wait for favorable winds
for her fearsome flight over the Gulf,
to safely reach the Florida peninsula,
where she comes every year to breed.

Once she finally arrives in spring,
to the Savannas Preserve on our coast,
daily we thrill to see her waltzing on high
and admire as she hunts on the wing.

These incredible birds are a treasure -
and if you have ever seen them fly,
you will understand why they stole my heart
when I first saw them dance in the sky.

Green Heron

Tiptoeing along the grassy edge
with cautious steps on crooked legs,

he stops to settle by the lake
and hunches his neck down.

Motionless and mute,
he stares blankly

toward the silent water,
as though lost in thought

like an old man in a dark suit
pondering his fate.

He stands a long time waiting,
waiting, as we all wait,

for something wondrous
to come along.

Rookery in Long Key Nature Park

An orange sun slides down
behind tall Sabal palms,
as evening sky is painted
with strands of tangerine.

Now from the west
while sunlight fades,
wave after white wave
of birds descend,

headed toward an ancient
errant tree, bent above
a small green pond,
the epicenter of rebirth.

Egrets, Herons, Ibis
arc down to rest
and feed the hungry mouths
hidden in deep nests.

Adult birds squabble,
shift and move,
in order to accommodate
the others coming late.

When night descends, the chicks
may dream of returning here
to mate and raise their young
in this familiar spot.

Cause and Effect

Sitting in the sun on
a cold January morning,
I randomly read
poems from a book

by Billy Collins.
So engrossed, I do
not realize how
still I have become

until a flash of Doves
alight close by
on the stepping stones
outside my porch.

My reading stopped,
I dare not move lest
they all fly off. Doves
are such nervous creatures,

perhaps because they
have so long been hunted
or food or sport,
although I put seeds out

for them while they watch
from atop our metal roof.
A slight move of my head,
one utters a small peep.

In concert now, the Doves
all dash away. Just as fast
I move to grab my pen and paper,
inspired to record all this.

Impending Storm Along the St Lucie River

Loose white clouds flee forward,
ahead of darkness
building on the south horizon.

Along the river's edge,
tall slash pines
begin to sway and bend.

Warning chirps exchanged, darting
Cardinals, Blue Jays, Mockingbirds
slip into the shrub.

Even the bold Red-Shouldered Hawk
repairs to a low branch
among the flexing pines.

Now the only bird aloft,
a Swallow-Tailed Kite,
soars in white waistcoat and black tails,

long wings outstretched,
gliding in ever higher circles,
loving the ride - before the storm arrives.

V

Resurrection

My daffodils spread charming yellow faces
too early, toward a warmly urging sun.
Slender stems grown tall,
with ruffled heads turned upward,
caught unaware and unprepared
to face a midnight frost

      when still so very young.

Once vibrant blooms trail down
shamefully to the ground,
while sister daffodils,
raised in more sheltered places,
unfold their shining beauty

      to slowly reach perfection.

Long standing trees above
wear scarves of tatted lace
and softly shake this filigree
of newly forming buds
to mourn in pious whispers

      the quick demise of early blooms.

But night cold has not killed their souls
locked well beneath the surface.
My daffodils will rise next year,
taller, straighter, stronger,
to mingle with the chorus
that sings in each new spring

      and have no shy regrets for anything.

Come Spend a Summer Afternoon with Me

Time can be bought in free fall flight,
suspended in the drowsy haze,
captured and held up in the light
of slowly moving summer days.

Watch butterflies waltz lightly by,
take time to hear the crickets trill.
See hawks rise up and spiral high,
listen now - as time stands still.

Look in the shade where pups doze there
upon the highest spot of ground,
to catch the slightest stir of air
should it begin to move around.

Notice squirrels chase up the trees,
sniff honeysuckle's sweet perfume
and in the hesitating breeze,
watch bees drift from bloom to bloom.

Gaze at a bluebird as he lands
lightly on a slender branch
that dips and rises as he stands,
while wind designs his random dance.

Lie down now in the cool green grass
to study clouds that move and change
and see again the pictures pass,
once thought lost with childhood games.

Walk down along the emerald cove
where a bass throws silver spray,
to leave white circles where he dove
that widen as he swims away.

Follow swallows while they weave
intricate patterns in their advance
on water bugs the birds retrieve
from a dangerous water dance.

Now shadows crawl across the dock
while gently time slides away,
uncounted by a ticking clock,
squandered on a soft green day.

Wildfire

An orange sun rose quickly in October,
high enough to hurl his rays
above the curve of this cold ball.

Sharp emblazoned beams pierced
the huddled woods with light
and struck the leaves aflame.

Saplings exploded in the glare,
tall trees caught rising fire -
each one burned a different shade.

Beech danced in yellow-gold,
dogwood blazed bold burgundy,
sweet gum flared with orange-ochre,

while the crinkled coppers of the oak
flickered till they shone, like polished
bottom cooking pots above an open flame.

The old dark green of quiet pines,
stood tall above this raging pyre,
knowing this cacaphony of color

would finally fall upon the forest floor.

Dangerous Season

Fall night air has drawn
moisture from the earth
and torn the dampness
into shreds of gauze,
that hang above the fallow fields
in the warming morning hours.

I come upon a young buck,
devouring tender shoots
along the roadway's edge.
Startled, he lifts his regal head
to stare, snagging glints
of sunlight on his fresh diadem.

He freezes at my close approach,
then bolts and bounds across my path,
clearing the barbed wire fence
with a flying grand jeté.

Leap by leap, he arcs across the meadow -
so light, his hooves leave no print of flight.

Run, young Prince!
Take refuge in the pines.
This is a dangerous season for freedom.

Autumn in Florida

Now residing in a tropic clime,
    I miss the northern fall,
    when yellow mums glow gold
    and orange pumpkins shine,
    where the Japanese Maple tree,
    with boughs curved down like dancer's arms,
    turns crimson in the slanted light.

Here, there is no morning fog
    to gently float above the still warm earth,
    and provide some moisture to extend
    the blooming lives of goldenrod.

I miss the sheen of late day sun,
    that made the autumn colors stun.
    Gone the scent of hearth fires in crisp air,
    underfoot the crunch of fallen leaves,
    painted trees reflected in peaceful ponds -
    and the single vision of an amber leaf,
    caught on pebbles in a slowly drifting stream.

Autumn never made me think of death,
    but rather life; the issuing of new seeds,
    rejuvenation of leaves preparing to compost,
    waiting for the new spring growth.
    Fall seems to be the shedding of old ideas,
    when, after winter's rest,
    fresh concepts will appear next year.

But year round here, the palm trees look the same,
    only the calendar tells me October's name.

Continuum

Low November fog
rolls above an icy shoreline,
lofting like a comforter
shaken out to loose its down.

A thread of Tundra Swans
slips from this swirling cover,
embroidering the air
above a hem of foam laced water.

The white thread rises,
going ragged in a headwind.
One by one the Swans stretch out,
stitched evenly for their long flight south.

The weary leader drops back
to the end of their wafting line,
to rest awhile in the draw
of deep white wings that beat before him.

Now a new leader
pulls this thread along,
weaving those wild Swans back
into the fabric of the fog.

VI

Philadelphia May 1945

Last week I turned four. Honeysuckle grows on the garage
in our backyard, winding upward like Jack's beanstalk. My
brother is three years older and shows me how to suck out
the sweet nectar.

When Mother has ladies come to our home, she sends me up
to nap. She says they must roll bandages to give to the Red
Cross, for The War. Quietly I sit at the top of the stairs, to
watch long sheets of gauze cut and rolled.

Father is rarely home. He did not go to The War. He is an
engineer busy making bombs for The War. Every day I
watch Blimps drift across the sky. I don't know why they are
up there, or why they are called Blimps, a very funny name.

One day my brother runs to me shouting, "Good News! The
War is over! Come on - there's a parade up the hill at the
end of the street!" I must take my little leather purse full of
saved pennies. I run inside to find it, while my brother waits
stomping his foot.

I follow him quickly up the hill but I trip on the gnarled
root of a tree grown over the sidewalk. I fall, spilling all
my pennies. He urges me to come, but I must pick up my
pennies. By then, my brother is gone. I am too little to go on
alone.

In the distance I can hear the squeak and thump of a band.
Our neighbors rush past me, cheering "The War is over!" I
stand abandoned. I do not understand the relief and joy on
their faces.

I scuff the ground with my shoes, turn around and return to
the safety of the honeysuckle.

Egypt's Hill

I was probably ten years old
when I heard of an exotic place
friends spoke about in whispers.

Our mothers warned us not to go
but of course we huffed our way
on fat-tire bikes past ordered lawns,

up the long straight rising road
until we ran out of pavement,
then pushed ahead through gravel.

We found a huge wide open land
of clay and loamy soil,
the first stage of new homes.

Someone had named it Egypt's Hill,
a massive area of loose earth
pushed and pulled by excavators.

Red mud was raked by earth movers
and imprinted with a plaid
woven by bulldozer treads.

Piles of dirt stood like pyramids,
clumps of dredged up trees lay down
just waiting to be climbed upon.

We fought the snakes that were their roots
and later rode their boughs like horses,
'cowboys and indians' was the game.

This place to us was heaven-sent,
where we could climb up high
to view the entire surrounding plain.

We imagined it a desert,
with nomadic tents, a green oasis
and a long camel train.

Covered in dirt arriving home,
our mothers must have known
where we had gone,

yet could never know
how great our adventure had been.

The Portrait

Hotel Dirigo, Southwest Harbor, Mt. Desert Island, Maine 1953
"The fish that we serve here today
slept last night in Frenchman's Bay"

I was twelve - she seventy-three,
an artist who also summered there.[1]
Mother sent me to sit for her,
so patiently I posed in a painted wicker chair

on the shiny green veranda of the Hotel Dirigo,
perched on the timeless coast of Maine.

While I sat, she scratched and smudged
her charcoal and pastels.
She rose to move my chin a bit,
chatting as she worked.
"Commissioned my dear," she said proudly.
"A birthday present for his wife."[2]

"Secretly he sat for me –
a handsome man he was you know,[3]
he never should have married her
and given up the throne!"

My portrait complete, I stared at it.
There I saw my mother's face.

Gazing at the portrait now
I view a girl from long ago,
with bright young eyes who could not see
how short her mother's life would be.

[1] Virginia Keep Clark
[2] Wallis Simpson
[3] King Edward VIII

Her Blue Dress

New Year's Day 1962.
Mother found lying on the floor,
the fear that struck me numb.

I phoned for help.
Father standing by,
unbelieving, shocked and mute.

At the hospital the doctors
telling us "a brain aneurysm,
there is nothing we could do."

Later I was told to choose
a dress for her to wear.
I could not find the blue one,

that matched her sparkling eyes,
until I remembered she wore
that dress the day she died.

Instead I chose a gold dress with
pearl buttons from neck to waist.
At her funeral hundreds came

to say, "she was so young..only fifty-one..
so kind..so sweet..a good friend.."
In the overpowering scent of flowers,

"Thank you," is all that I could answer.
As I approached the coffin
and saw her lying there,

the blue dress no longer mattered,
for her loving blue eyes now
were closed forever.

Legacies

I remember little girls
with overblown bonnets and puffed up skirts,
all cut from a single pattern of pastel calicoes.
Each walked the same direction
upon a ground of white,
fixed forever in separate squares
divided by pale green bands.

Each square was quilted into place
by my mother's grandmother's hands.

After Mother died so very suddenly,
it never occurred to me
to ask for anything
that had belonged to her.
My father's heart was broken.
Time healed him fast
and he was married

to a redhead in a purple dress.
Then of course I could not ask.

Ten years later I inquired
the whereabouts of the puffed up girls.
He said he hadn't seen the quilt
for many years.
Last month he told me he'd given away
my mother's mother's wicker chairs
to the daughter of his red haired wife.

Alone in bed, I shed my mask
and cried like a child that night.

I bought three old quilts recently.
Two have patchwork squares of pastel calicoes,
one has a star design framed with bands of green.
I expect I will buy more though I have no use for them.
I have no daughters of my own - only two wonderful sons.
Perhaps someday my sons
will have daughters of their own.

At least I could pass on these quilts
to them when they are grown.

Solutions

When my two blond boys were young,
they played with Olga's dark haired son.
One day Scott came home to me,
eyes wide with questioning.

"Otto's Mother catches squirrels and holds them
in a box, underneath the car exhaust 'til all their

scratching stops – Why does she do that?"
I saw the traps set all about our backdoor neighbor's lot.

Maple branches reached and stretched
across the boundaries of our sub-divided plots.
To rid her yard of squirrels, she'd have to catch
the rest in town – the state – the world!

My boys were endlessly delighted
by these daring acrobats, fed them
in the winter – seeds and peanut butter
when they looked thinner.

They watched these lively creatures with startled eyes,
who fiercely struggled to survive – maybe even learned
a lesson from their instinct to store acorns they would need,
when our oak trees held no more.

I tried to teach my sons to be good boys
and not touch things that were not theirs.
But I cheered them silently next day,
when looking out the back,

I saw two blond-haired boys
creep from trap to trap,
unhooking each little door
and opening every latch.

The Gift

The Christmas present
arrived on my doorstep,
from my husband's sister.

Unwrapped, I found an afghan
she had made, exactly the match
of blue-grey color on the bedroom

walls in our new home - a home
she had never seen. How could
she know it was the perfect shade?

I imagined her knitting
her gifts that year,
much like the Greek Fates of myth

who wove destiny
into the fabrics they made.
Was she weaving the inevitable?

Ten months later the thread was cut,
she passed away - too young, too beautiful.
Oh, how I miss her.

How could she have known
how comforting her afghan
would be, wrapped around me

in my sorrow?

Her Garden at Twilight
Elegy For Cathy

She goes to her garden at twilight
to watch the slanted shafts
of sunlight fading slowly
on the fountain wall,

yet lighting liquid diamonds still
where water droplets splash.

She studies jasmine's arabesques
as tendrils twist out searching
something to hold on to,

until they loosely droop
and catch upon themselves.

She hears the evening chatter
of the roosting birds
discuss their sleeping spaces,

then with gentle murmurs
tuck their heads and disappear.

She feels cicadas' rhythms
as the nightly song begins,
soon joined by croaking frogs

who send unanswered notes of love,
their voices like plucked strings.

She finds the secret places
beside the painted fern,
or on the backs of fireflies,

among the wilted roses
where lost memories reside.

She lingers in her garden while
night paints the greens in shades of black
to hold these last few moments
before the stars race past.

Then whispering good-bye,
she slips into the darkness with a sigh.

The Ballad of Richard Prouty

Richard was born the youngest son
so would not inherit wealth;
that was left to the eldest one,
Richard must fend for himself.

At fourteen he dared to make a plan,
traveled to Bristol to find
a ship outbound for new free land
and leave England behind.

In 1647 on a crowded ship,
he crossed the Atlantic alone
landing at Plymouth Colony,
his fortune still unknown.

He reported to Lieutenant James Torry
offering to help defend
the fortress from frequent Indian attacks
hoping to gain a friend.

Armed with a musket he bravely fought
(Perhaps that way he might meet
the Lieutenant's beautiful daughter;
seeing her made his heart beat.)

Richard and Demaris later wed,
with four children they were endowed.
Given acreage in Situate, Massachusetts
for his service, made Richard very proud.

Looking back at my family history
ten generations ago,
I find I am a true American
and now I finally know,

I owe my existence to Richard's daring
to come to America and stay.
I learned his story from a genealogy book -
that I carry his DNA.

VII

Rejuvenation

A week past winter solstice
I stepped into my southern garden,
startled suddenly by a
black snake very close to me.

He was startled too, and quickly
turned his lifted head away.
Silently I slipped back on my porch
to watch what he would do.

Finally he slithered off
through the unmown grass,
sprinkled with a thousand diamonds
from the morning dew.

Later I went out again
to find out why he'd come
and discovered he had shed his skin;
a perfect negative of him

rested near my flowerpot.
The New Year ready to begin,
how wonderful to be renewed
and leave all vestiges behind -

sadness, failure, remorse, regret,
anger, jealousy and sin,
to start afresh, newly cleansed,
shiny black and eager to begin again.

A Buzzing in My Ear

Sitting on the porch
with my morning
cup of coffee,
I see a yellow bee
with folded wings
crawling frantically
across my closed
screen door.

Was she locked inside,
or outside
just exploring?

Moving closer
to inspect,
yet never asking
this insect if she were
the African or
Honey type of bee,
I opened up the door
so I could set her free -

She hesitated,
as if she did not know
she could now go
to finish up her work.
Finally she flew,
humming a little tune,
stopping briefly for a taste
of nectar from a nearby bloom.

Searching for a Safe Place

Pouring rain falls like a veil
around my covered porch.
Hidden from the outside world
amid this deluge, I stay dry

and observe a fat toad, bouncing
like a small dark leather ball
along the wet edge of my deck,
hoping to find shelter.

He moves past a tiny singing frog
clinging to the wall,
a different species - yet a neighbor,
also seeking refuge.

The fat toad hops on toward
the end of the deck, but stops
to contemplate my bar-b-que,
shielded in its black raincoat.

Thinking better of it, he jumps
into my narrow garden,
where the self-propagating ferns
hold the promise of protection.

Night Music

A tribe of frogs sends tom-tom cries
of love across the lake -
they wait, listening for an answer,
while the waning moon slips slowly
behind a bank of clouds.

Dancing stars slide closer
through a quiet sky,
to wink upon the mirror lake,
as the spring night throbs again.

The whole world sleeps
this hushed late hour; no soul awake
to feel night's warm embrace -
no sound nor sign of life,
save the frogs' persistent pleas

and me.

Luna Moth

"I found a fairy, REALLY – come quick and look!"

His parents never heard as they laughed and talked.
Grampa was busy filling in his crossword,
while his sister rolled her eyes, returning to her book.
Our cabin stood alone atop a mountain
in the blackness of a summer night.
My grandson led me to his bedroom.
We sat together in the dark - half a century apart -
staring out his window at a solitary light,
quietly awaiting for the fairy to return.
Was he thinking of lost teeth, or stories read aloud?

Midnight moths twirled and flipped about,
turning golden as they neared the light.
A bat swooped through the crowd
to snatch a gilded dancer in mid-flight.

"Just wait – she WILL come back!"

Suddenly his magical green fairy reappeared,
larger than the others with flowing golden hair,
long slender legs and lacy wings of palest green.
She hovered near the spotlight, while all around
the small ones danced and dipped in courtly fashion,
paying homage to the Fairy Queen.
Who knows how long she kept us in her spell -
until she flew off into the forest where all fairies dwell.
His nine-year-old eyes shone with wonder,
as he turned toward me and smiled.

A thought came unbidden from deep inside my mind.

I see a mountain stream – a stone gristmill – a wooden water wheel
and at the bottom of the wheel, where the water falls,
overhung with rhododendron, a pool of deepest blue.

And there among the bubbles, I once saw fairies too.

The Prize

On our way to the town of Due West,
(a pinprick on the map)
we follow a ribbon of road
running through low cotton fields
stunted by South Carolina clay.
We ride past small lonely farms,
never seeing the hunger inside.

Our destination is a country fair,
set back in time on a fallow field.
No Ferris wheel or mechanical rides,
just cows and chickens with blue ribbons,
a kissing booth with giggly girls,
fresh peaches for sale
and sweet potato pies.

At two o'clock, in a temporary pen,
a greased pig contest is set to begin.
A group of barefoot kids,
all under the age of ten,
excitedly wait to catch the pig,
who appears to be quite slippery
with lard slathered all over his skin.

Round behind the pig they race.
At every grab, the kids slide off
to land abruptly in the dust.
A thin little boy in ragged jeans
catches the pig's back leg.
Hands tightly clasped, he holds on fast
until the pig gives in.

We watch this little guy, eyes wide,
stand proudly beside the judge
to wait announcement of the prize.
Perhaps it's just for fun
or maybe the prize is cash.
His parents and brothers pull up
in a rusted old farm truck.

While the pig is loaded in,
the young boy wears a shining grin,
a smile now shared by all of them.

Constancy

I cannot now recall
why my need to wander
out to view our pond at that late hour -
perhaps to check the water level
for the fish that steamy summer night.
Walking to the garden
down the old stone steps,
my left foot slipped
on the mossy dew-wet stone.
My leg was caught and held
between the post and step.
Like a twig it broke with three small snaps.
Within a web of pain, I called out for aid.

My faint cries muffled
by the humid August air,
I crawled up the grassy slope
slowly on my knees,
toward the lighted kitchen door.
At last he heard my voice -
like a whirlwind
picked me up
and whisked me to the car.
Before we sped away
I saw behind the open kitchen door
my beagle standing still,
a puzzled look upon her face.

All night he stayed and waited
through x-rays and the surgery,
then the long return
from misty anesthesia.
When he finally ascertained
it was all right to leave,
he returned alone back to our home
as the sun began to rise -
to find the beagle standing there,
just as she was before,
still watching from behind
the open kitchen door.

The Natural Line
Ninety-Six, South Carolina

Through evening's dusky light, I gaze
across my new mown lawn and
at the edge, I see at once a line is drawn.

Beyond my tended property, lies a
dark and tangled wood, left many years
at liberty for vines to twine and creep.

What mysteries might hide
behind the natural line of pines
and water oaks bent free?

Green butterflies with folded wings,
the shadow of a high-stepped fox,
a black snake coiling in the leaves.

The great horned owl on stealthy wings,
floating through the angled trees,
searching for his evening meal.

Chipmunks, voles and mice,
burrowing in their holes, to hide
and wait for safer daylight hours.

A bobcat's startling lovesick scream,
that wakes wild turkeys where they roost
in branches of a darkened bush.

Hurried bats who deftly fly
in the black night air, guided
by the music only they can hear.

And perhaps beneath an ancient apple tree,
the echo of old souls, who once tamed
this primal land three hundred years ago.

Signs

A missed sign, a wrong turn
and I'm driving my
small red convertible
beside clean, white board fences.

Scanning the sweet smelling fields,
I search for grazing horses.

Suddenly stopped by a sharp right turn,
terrified, I face a huge black bull in front,
up against a three board fence.

The bull snorts steam in the morning air,
while I stare into his fiery black eyes,
set beneath two large curved horns
borrowed straight from the devil.

Hypnotized by this behemoth,
who could easily break the fence
with merely a step or two,
I sit very still behind the wheel.

Observing, I begin to see him as a sign,
confronted, as a Native American
might be, viewing her own totem.

Soon his snorting subsides, dark eyes
soften and I almost feel befriended.

Perhaps somehow this bull now knew,
I am a Taurus too.

A Heart Too Big

Pumpkin was our beagle
of silky ears and gentle licks.
Her deep brown eyes were filled
with trust and honesty.

Often she seemed telepathic,
if I thought about a walk,
quickly up - she would head
directly to the door.

One morning in late summer
I awakened with a start,
to find sweet Pumpkin at my feet
lying stiffly on her quilted bed.

Only nine years old,
she had a heart too big,
which could not last forever.
(Our Vet had told me that).

We buried her behind the barn
where the soil was rich and soft;
though summer now was almost gone
the earth still held some warmth.

I picked the last flowers blooming
from my fading garden bed
to place atop the little mound
beneath where Pumpkin laid.

Our other beagle, Peaches,
sniffed all around that spot,
knowing Pumpkin had been there,
not understanding she was gone.

Just then, against the shining sky,
a dark V of geese appeared,
heading toward the old red barn
winging high above the field.

They flew in perfect form,
gliding lower as they neared,
to pass in silent tribute -
directly overhead.

VIII

Ascension

Dusk descended into evening,
a few fireflies awoke,
drifting low above the grass
to glow upon forget-me-nots.

As the night sky darkened
on an early summer's eve,
more fireflies were floating up
to glimmer in the trees.

Before the moon arose
countless fireflies arrived,
soon there was no place
that did not sparkle with their light.

When the earth was hushed
and all the stars appeared,
the fireflies flew higher
than I had ever seen before.

I stood bereft and lonely
as I watched them rise,
until I could no longer tell
the stars from fireflies.

Futility in Three-Quarter Time

The fan blades above me
    turn faster,
around and around and around.

Like my mind as it runs
    from disaster,
unable to stop or slow down.

This dilemma wraps tightly
    around me,
I feel my heart starting to pound.

My life now unravels
    like kite string,
that tangles and can't be rewound.

Ideas fly out chasing
    dark shadows,
old mistakes echo back and resound.

Endless circles of thought
    search for answers,
solutions that cannot be found.

While the fan up there just keeps
    on turning,
around and around and around.

Reflections on a Morning

Bright sun lights up
the low landscape, reflecting
golden homes on the quiescent lake.

A breeze gently stirs the palms,
fluttering fronds
to a slowly swaying Samba.

Lunging upward, a hungry
fish creates a wake
and now the water changes.

Upside-down houses on the lake,
bits of gold and terracotta,
become paintings by Seurat.

Water moves in cross-hatched lines
shifting pictures to points of light,
melding gold with blue and green.

Clouds emerge, wind swells, the water
morphs to silver grey. Awake, now
the lake marches onward in small waves.

The clarity of morning diffused,
inexorably, we now move forward -
and so another day begins.

Fall Slips Into Florida

An afternoon arrives in late August
and the earth tilts slightly.

The burn of southern sun lessens
as tree shadows slowly stretch

their fingers farther across the yard.
A flight of swallows dips and glides,

cleansing the air of insects rising
above the field. The sun sets and

coral clouds melt into a sky of navy,
while a bunny lopes across the grass

to find sleep in the bed
of my Mexican petunias.

The quiet night slides down
around me softly, like a coverlet.

I'm told a tropical wave
threatens from far out at sea;

but for now, I only feel
peace and tranquility.

One More Day

We do not often contemplate
our own mortality.

Only when we hesitate,
in the last quarter of our lives,

and stop to take the time
to observe ephemeral clouds arise,

or raise our heads to a starlit sky.
If we think it all might end tomorrow,

even then we sigh
and brush these thoughts away

to still make plans for the following year,
next month, next week, next day,

but to ourselves we say –
we would always wish to have

only just one more day.

about the author

Judith L. Shaffer was born and grew up in Westfield, NJ. She has lived in seven different states since getting married. Judy has held numerous jobs: Director of the Westfield United Fund, member of the Planning Boards of both Westfield, NJ and Nags Head, NC, owner of four retail shops in Nags Head and General Manager of a custom order furniture store in Maryland. Judy attended Lander University, majoring in English, and also studied with Bennie Lee Sinclair, Poet Laureate of South Carolina. She is a past member of the Fort Lauderdale Writers' Group and presently a member of the Morningside Writer's Group in Port St. Lucie, Florida.

Judy has had several poems published in *Midwest Poetry Review*. Her poem "Last Night" won 4th prize in a national contest. "Dangerous Season" was published and Judy was selected as the best new poet of the month in January 1990 by *Midwest Poetry Review*. Her poem "Elegy for Cathy" won 1st prize in the Writers' Network of South Florida 2012 Poetry Contest. *Behind the Blue Edge of the Sea* is Judy's first book of poems.

Judy and her husband, Larry, are retired and live in Port St. Lucie, FL. Larry has just published his first novel, *Water Oaks Revelation*, a mystery, a love story, with an added dose of science fiction.

You can reach Judy at judyshaffer2@gmail.com

acknowledgements

I wish to thank all the members of the Morningside Writer's Group for being my sounding board and for their suggestions and support, as well as my husband, who is so kind to think everything I write is good! Also a grateful thank you to Kris Haggblom, my publisher, for his advice and assistance getting this book into print.

colophon

Behind the Blue Edge of the Sea, by Judith L. Shaffer,
was set with **Trebuchet MS** and **Palatino Linotype** fonts
by SpiNDec, Port Saint Lucie, Florida

CPSIA information can be obtained
at www.ICGtesting.com
Printed in the USA
FSHW020728250120
66349FS